Identity Theft - A Growth Industry

For some time now, identity theft has been almost universally acknowledged as the fastest-growing crime in the nation, if not the world. So much personal information is now available about the Average Joe that criminals have turned identity theft into an all-you-eat buffet. They drape themselves in your good name and reputation, and - like some evil twin - create havoc in the guise of your person, for which you are wrongfully blamed.

However, there are still things you can do to avoid being a victim, as well as regain control after being victimized. This book, in a quick and easy fashion, will show you the steps to take in order to best your evil twin.

Besting Your Evil Twin: A Simple Guide to Battling Identity Theft

BESTING YOUR EVIL TWIN

A Simple Guide to Battling Identity Theft - Before and After It Happens

By

S.A. Wilson

Besting Your Evil Twin: A Simple Guide to Battling Identity Theft

This book is published by I&H Recherche Publishing.

ISBN: 978-1-937666-02-6

Printed in the U.S.A.

Besting Your Evil Twin: A Simple Guide to Battling Identity Theft

CONTENTS

Besting Your Evil Twin: A Simple Guide to Battling Identity Theft

ACKNOWLEDGMENTS

I would like to thank GOD, who granted me both a love of reading and writing, and put me in a position to be able to share my insignificant thoughts with the world; my family, who have always given me the love and support I needed; and my teachers through all grades and at all institutions, who always encouraged my writing and helped my development as an author.

Besting Your Evil Twin: A Simple Guide to Battling Identity Theft

DISCLAIMER

The subject matter of this book, as presented, is not and was never intended to be, serve as, or be interpreted as legal advice. Anyone seeking a legal opinion on the matters discussed herein is advised to consult with legal counsel. In addition, this book does not indicate every conceivable action that could be taken to prevent or combat identity theft.

Besting Your Evil Twin: A Simple Guide to Battling Identity Theft

Thank you for purchasing this book. If you found it helpful or enlightening, please feel free to leave a review on the site from which it was purchased.

For additional information on identity theft – including how to combat it and recover from it – please visit my website, Identity Theft Defense HQ, located here: http://www.identitytheftdefensehq.com/

Besting Your Evil Twin: A Simple Guide to Battling Identity Theft

Besting Your Evil Twin: A Simple Guide to Battling Identity Theft

PROLOGUE

A few years ago, a colleague had the misfortune of having her identity stolen. Of course, she didn't know this right away. By its very nature, identity theft is a subtle crime and difficult to detect initially. In fact, several weeks passed before my friend realized that there was an issue. The problem only came to light after she had a check bounce, despite the fact that she believed she had more than enough funds on deposit to cover it. As you might guess, the thieves had cleaned out her bank account. Even worse, they had gone on to obtain credit in her name and were busy racking up additional charges on a daily basis.

Needless to say, it was a nightmare of epic proportions. It was an on-going battle as my friend constantly found herself on the defensive - calling banks, creditors, etc., trying to explain the situation - while the thieves continually opened new lines of credit in her name. In short, she had to take a leave of absence from work for six months in order to get her life back, so to speak. But the worst thing about it may be simply the way that it happened. My friend wasn't particularly careless with her personal information and didn't take unnecessary risks; she did everything as she normally did and didn't vary from her routine. However, at one of the places where she usually pays with a check, some unscrupulous person copied her banking information from the check and then simply began printing checks on her account with check-writing software.

Sadly, this is a typical story for those who have had their identity stolen. On my part, my knowledge of this topic first came by virtue of working for a client who had an identity theft issue but didn't have the time to deal with it personally. He gave me the authority to address the matter, and, over the course of the next year, I was able to satisfactorily resolve all of the issues - learning along the way the best ways to go about protecting oneself from identity theft. It is these practice tips, which are pretty simple but amazingly effective, that I have shared with others since then and now share with you. Hopefully they will serve to prevent you from becoming a victim of identity theft, or get back on your feet in short order if you do.

PART I PREVENTION
Batten Down the Hatches
(Steps to Take Before Anything Happens)

In most situations in life, it pays to be proactive. For instance, if there's a particular job you want, you usually have to apply for it; rarely will someone just offer it to you. If you want to dance with the prettiest girl at the ball, you have to ask her rather than wait for her to approach you. Likewise, when it comes to the subject of identity theft, you (as the potential victim) will be far better off if you take the initiative in terms of preventing this crime as opposed to trying to fix it afterwards.

Identity theft is considered to be the fastest-growing crime in the nation, if not the world. With that in mind, no one can afford to cross their fingers, tuck their head in the sand, and simply hope that it doesn't happen to them. You can rest assured that the criminals in this arena aren't waiting to just get lucky; they are actively pursuing your information, hoping to get enough of your personal data to cloak themselves in your name and financial image. Then, like some evil twin, they set about convincing the world that they are you, creating havoc and leaving you to deal with the fallout.

The concept of an evil twin has been prevalent in fiction for decades: the hero of the story is living a somewhat charmed existence, when - for no apparent reason - things start to go very, very wrong. He is accused of being in places where he has not been, and is seen by witnesses committing acts he did not do. Slowly, the protagonist comes to realize that another person is committing these acts for which he is being blamed. Someone who looks just like him, but without the same moral compass. An evil twin.

Essentially, this is what identity thieves do. They hold themselves out as someone else, and then proceed to ruin that person's good name and reputation in order to achieve their own ends. However, there are things you can do to protect yourself from fraud of this nature. There are steps you can take that will make it more difficult for your own evil twin to come into existence, but you have to be proactive, as noted in Chapters 1-4 of this book, to prevent this from occurring. Later, should your preventive methods prove unsuccessful, we'll address how you can regain control after your identity has been compromised.

Chapter 1 Monitoring - An Ounce of Prevention is Worth a Pound of Cure

Someone once said that, in order to be successful, every criminal needs at least one essential element for his crime: opportunity. Leaving your keys running in the ignition, forgetting to lock the door to your house, leaving your purse unattended... These are all examples of ways in which thieves are granted an opportunity to carry on in their chosen profession. The first step in denying them that, in terms of identity theft, is monitoring. Simply put, you have to constantly be on guard for things that are suspicious or out of the ordinary in relation to your personal and financial information, e.g.:

(i) Credit cards - Go over your statements carefully. Make sure that you are aware of and familiar with all charges and/or vendors. If anything appears unfamiliar, do not hesitate to investigate, whether it be calling the credit card company for more information or disputing the charge. Also, you are entitled to a free copy of your credit report each year from the three major credit-reporting agencies - Equifax, TransUnion and Experian. Thus, you can request one of the three reports every four months, thereby regularly checking your credit history. These free annual reports can be obtained online at the following: https://www.annualcreditreport.com.

(ii) Bank accounts - As with credit cards, you should scrutinize all payments and withdrawals. If you're lucky, your bank may also be one of those that tracks unfamiliar purchases or spending patterns and contacts you for confirmation. (My bank does this as standard policy.) Also, after making a withdrawal from an ATM, keep an eye on your account for the next day or two afterwards. ATMs are a prime target for identity thieves with respect to getting your personal information.

(iii) Mail - This is probably where you are most vulnerable to identity theft, so there's a two-fold assignment here: you're being vigilant to ensure that (a) you're getting mail in general, and (b) you're getting specific mail items when due, such as utility bills, bank statements, etc.

To be frank, anyone can send in a change-of-address form and have your mail forwarded elsewhere. Fortunately, junk mail is so prevalent these days that, even on occasions when we receive nothing important, most of us get mail of some sort. This is a positive in the sense of indicating that your mail probably hasn't been tampered with from the standpoint of being redirected elsewhere. (And you thought junk mail served no purpose and was just....well, junk.)

Thus, unless it is typical of you not to get mail daily, any day on which no mail is delivered should probably be a red flag. If there's a second consecutive day without mail, klaxons should be going off in your brain, and you should call your local post office to see if there's a problem. Personally - excluding Sundays and holidays - I don't recall a single day over at least the past 10 years on which I did not receive mail of any kind. However, I do recall on one occasion that I did not receive any mail for two consecutive days, so, quite alarmed, I called the local post office and was relieved to find out that the first day with no mail had been a holiday - Columbus Day - and all of the carriers were running well behind on their routes (and would be quite late) the second day, which was also the day I called.

> With respect to specific mail items, you should have a rough estimate of when bills and financial statements are due to arrive and become suspicious if they are late. I started tracking mail of this sort many moons ago, not because of identity theft (which was not as widespread back then) but because I was charged a late fee by a creditor for a bill that I never received. Since then, I've always had a close estimate of when bills, financial statements and the like are due to arrive.

In brief, monitoring is the first line of defense. Take it seriously, because this is often where the battle gets won or lost - sometimes before it even begins. To help on this front, some people also choose to employ a credit-monitoring service. Such services often provide an extra level of comfort and additional peace of mind, but are certainly not required to adequately scrutinize your credit and spending for illicit activity.

Chapter 2 Shredding - The Best Offense is a Good Defense

The next step in our battle to fight identity theft is probably the simplest to understand and implement: invest in a good shredder. And use it.

What's a good shredder? I would recommend a cross-cut shredder (sometimes called a cross shredder), which will cut documents into small pieces. This will make it more difficult to reconstruct the document than if you used a strip-cut shredder (which, as the name implies, merely cuts documents into strips). I would also recommend a shredder that will take multiple sheets of paper - something like eight or so - at a time, as well as staples and possibly even credit cards. Otherwise, you may find yourself spending quite a bit of time in front of the shredder feeding it a single page at a time, *after* removing any staples. (I learned this lesson the hard way, first buying a cheap, single-page shredder and then only upgrading about one feature - multiple pages, staples, etc. - at a time. The end result is that we now have about 3 shredders lying around the house unused because the 4th and final shredder is the only one that does everything we need.)

On a side note, although one would think that it shouldn't bear mentioning, I would be remiss if I didn't point out that if you purchase a shredder to help protect your identity, please, Please, PLEASE use it! Many people who buy shredders for this purpose consistently fail to utilize them. These individuals continue exercising the same age-old habit of just throwing their mail and other documents in the trash, or they find shredding to be a bore (and let's face it: *Indiana Jones* it's not) and soon abandon the practice. Nevertheless, I encourage you to make shredding part of your daily routine, as it is one of the best ways to deny your evil twin an opportunity to mask himself in your likeness. Failing to do so is like buying an anti-theft device for your car and never putting it to use: although using it probably doesn't guarantee that your vehicle won't get stolen, it makes it a lot less likely.

The next question, of course, is *what* should you shred. Personally, I believe that you should shred anything that has your name and/or address on it that you don't plan to keep, because those two bits of information are often starting points for identity theft. This category of items will, for the most part, consist of mail, including junk mail, credit card offers, charitable requests, etc. However, this might also include other items, such as early versions of documents you drafted, letters, misfeeds or misprints from the printer, what have you. (To be truthful, however, there ways to get your name/address that don't require a thief to physically get his hands on your mail or the like. Still, there's no need in making it easy for him.)

In addition, you should also shred any documents containing critical information (e.g., account numbers, social security numbers, passwords, account balances, and so on). Basically, anything you would not want a stranger (or even some relatives) to know. A good litmus test is this: *Would I be concerned if a stranger on the street found this document?* If you can't answer that question with an immediate, resounding, unequivocal "No" then you should probably shred the document.

Finally, as noted above, you absolutely must shred or destroy credit cards and debit cards, even if they are beyond the expiration date. This is one area in which a friend of mine is particularly paranoid: he cuts old credit cards into small pieces with a pair of scissors and then separates them into three piles. The first pile gets flushed down the toilet; the second gets tossed into the trash; the third pile gets tossed into the trash can of a nearby gas station the next time he goes there. Not everyone will feel the need to go as far as my friend, but the point is that you should endorse a level of protection that you feel comfortable with and which will allow you to sleep at night.

Chapter 3 Communicating Electronically - Simplify Your Life

As you can probably tell from the first two chapters of this book, one of the more tedious details of preventing identity theft revolves around establishing control with respect to the amount of paper that people, in general, have to deal with on a regular basis. There is a vast amount of paperwork involved in our daily lives: receipts, applications, trial offers, account statements, what have you... The sheer volume of documents that relate to each of us is quite impressive - and can be overwhelming - when you really think about it.

However, what also becomes clearly evident is that we can reduce the likelihood of identity theft by reducing the amount of paper we regularly deal with. For instance, fewer bills received via regular mail means less opportunity for a criminal to obtain your personal information (and less paperwork for you to deal with in term of shredding, preserving, etc.).

Obviously then, one of the first things to do is to arrange to receive as much communication as possible electronically. This should include bank statements, utility bills, credit card statements - the works. Almost all financial institutions are now set up for electronic document delivery, and it's no secret that this is their preference, since they make a mint in savings from postal fees alone (not to mention paper and printing costs). The same is true for utility companies and other service providers, like cable companies.

Also, if you haven't done so already, sign up for electronic bill-paying. Most major banks now offer this service to their customers for free. In addition to removing another potential link in the identity-theft chain, it's just flat-out convenient, saving you the hassle of buying postage, dropping items in the mail, and the like. (Not to mention the amount of time it saves you, since you only have to enter payment information for a bill once.)

In brief, battling identity theft involves stepping out of the Stone Age and embracing technology. As odd as it sounds, doing so will actually simplify your life, saving you time and money as well as helping to keep identity thieves at bay.

Chapter 4 Eliminating Bad Habits

Let's be honest: even for those that have adopted the suggestions noted in the first three chapters, many people will still leave themselves open to identity theft just by virtue of having certain bad habits. There are particular behaviors that make you more prone to being a victim of identity theft than others, but it's more than possible to curb or eliminate those specific traits.

First of all, be discriminating in terms of the information that you reveal to other people. The advent of social media such as Facebook and Myspace has made it possible to connect and share with other people on more levels and in more ways than ever before. For instance, every week Facebook informs me which of my "Friends" (even those I've never met) has an upcoming birthday. It doesn't seem like much, but birth dates are one of those critical items that often help identify us, and as such that information is often targeted by identity thieves. Ergo, entering personal information, such as birth dates or addresses on social sites is not a very bright idea. By way of example, I was absolutely shocked when I first joined Facebook and saw that a relative had entered not only her correct birthday but other personal information. When I mentioned that she was probably making herself a target for identity theft, she quickly addressed the situation. (Frankly speaking, I rarely ever enter correct personal information on such sites, so I have little concern about others getting unauthorized access to it.

Thus, when a website that I occasionally visit was recently hacked and information regarding millions of users stolen, I still slept like a baby.)

Next, be wary of information you give out over cell phones and wireless phones. Our baby monitor used to pick up our calls from our neighbor's wireless phone all the time. Put plainly, these wireless methods of communication have, historically, been less secure than landlines, because intercepting the call merely required being on the same frequency. In short, identity thieves typically have not had as much trouble eavesdropping on a cell phone versus a traditional landline. Although there is much debate today about just how secure the current generation of cell phones are, discretion is the better part of valor. If you have to give out personal information via telephone, don't use a cell phone.

In addition, use caution when dealing with individuals who contact you and attempt to get any degree of personal information (assuming you did not initiate contact). This could be someone calling to offer you a new product or service, or someone claiming to represent a creditor seeking payment. For instance, a few years ago I received a phone call at my office from someone who purportedly represented a service provider seeking to be paid prior to sending an invoice. I didn't have an issue with making the payment early, but I refused to give the alleged representative any credit card information because, as I put it, I needed "some degree of comfort regarding the legitimacy of the request." Therefore, I called the service provider, who confirmed that they were indeed seeking early payment. Although there was nothing underhanded taking place in this instance, it could just as easily have been someone trying to get personal information from me that they could use to their advantage.

Be suspicious of changes in protocol or appearance when it comes to items you're familiar with, such as letters received from creditors, websites, etc. By way of example, my bank has made several changes to their website over the past few years, and with each noted alteration I always call the bank and confirm that the site has indeed been altered before logging in. Remember, one of the ways in which criminals capture your personal information is by sending you to a fake web site and inducing you to enter your login information and passwords.

Don't just toss away or ignore receipts. On many occasions, I've seen people at gas stations pay by credit card and then absentmindedly toss the receipt in the trash - when they don't just drive off without taking it at all. Likewise, people paying for a meal with a credit card or withdrawing money from an ATM will often just throw the receipt into the nearest trash receptacle. This is an extremely poor practice, because these little slips of paper sometimes contain critical bits of information. For instance, although they seldom contain a complete credit card number, receipts will often have a partial number (e.g., the last four digits), the type of card (for instance, Visa) and your name (or some variation thereof, such as a first initial and last name). Unless it's an absolute necessity, I wouldn't get a credit card receipt from a gas station pump. (I believe most modern pumps even give you the option of having a receipt printed or not.) With other receipts, it's probably best to take them home and shred them.

Finally, try to limit the number of checks that you actually write. Even if you switch to online bill-paying, you will probably be unable to escape check-writing altogether; there's always someone out there who is archaic in the sense of not taking credit cards - e.g., a small mom-and-pop bookstore or similar operation that's adverse to paying credit card merchant fees. Bearing this in mind, it might make sense to adopt a policy which I implemented several years ago for this very type of situation. Basically, I set up a second checking account that I use whenever I have to write a physical check. I usually keep very little money in it, so that should someone gain unauthorized access to it there will be little gain for them. (More to the point, your own liability is limited in such situations, but that will be discussed later in Part II.) Regardless, you should give checks the same treatment that you give to cash and credit cards in terms of security.

Frankly speaking, people in general seem to have several bad habits with respect to safeguarding their personal data. This isn't really because they are poor stewards of their own information; it's simply the fact that thieves have become more sophisticated, such that what was previously harmless behavior now bears the possibility of menace. This is a fact that will become only more prevalent as time passes, and we can fully expect that changes in criminal methodology will continually force law-abiding citizens to adapt accordingly.

PART II RECOVERY
Ride Out the Storm
(What to Do After Your Identity is Stolen)

So, the worst has happened: someone has stolen your identity. Now, cloaked in your your good name, they are - like an evil twin - busy causing you no end of headache and worry by masquerading as you.

There is however, a little bit of a silver lining here. First of all, your liability is usually limited when it comes to identity theft. You are only liable for up to $50 of charges on credit cards (provided you report the fraudulent charges within 60 days). Similarly, your liability for purchases made with a lost/stolen debit card is limited to $50, but only if reported within two business days of the incident. If reported between 2 and 60 days from the date of the incident, your liability is limited to $500. Beyond 60 days there is no limit to your liability. (This harkens back to one of the key tenets of identity theft prevention: monitoring.)

After the theft occurs, you will be fighting a war on several fronts - namely, preventing further abuse and protecting your good name (i.e, your credit rating). Part II of this book outlines the steps you should take to get things back on track.

Chapter 5 Report the Theft to the Police

Without question, you need to file a police report if your identity has been compromised. While it is debatable whether this should be the *very* first step - only calling your bank and creditors might rank higher - you will eventually need to do so because a valid police/incident report will be required at some point by almost all financial institutions and credit card issuers to whom you report the theft of your identity. This is, to some extent, intended to ensure that your claim of identity theft is true, as opposed your trying to get out of obligations you've incurred. (Remember: your liability in these instances is limited by law, and many people see that as an opportunity to take advantage of the system.) Moreover, the three major credit reporting agencies will require this report as well.

Investigation of the crime is likely to be handled by the Financial Crimes Division of your local police department. Be sure to make a copy of the Incident Report, as your creditors and financial institutions will most likely ask for such. (You'll also want a copy for your own records.) Even if they do not ask for the report itself, they will often request that you provide other information - such as the Incident Report number or the name of the officer in charge of the investigation - so that they can obtain pertinent information through their own channels rather than rely on you. (Simply put, if you are trying to defraud your creditors, it would be unwise of them to ask you to provide a copy of the

Incident Report, as you might manufacture the document yourself.)

Many times, the victims of identity theft are surprised to learn that the person stealing their identity is actually a friend or relative. (To a certain extent, this makes sense in that these are the people who often have access to our personal information.) In such instances, the question of whether to pursue formal charges becomes rather delicate. For instance, one young man consulting with me on this issue revealed that the person who had stolen his identity was his mother. He was torn between trying to repair the damage she had done to his name and credit, and trying to find a way to stop her short of pressing charges. For those of you who find yourselves in a similar situation, it sometimes comes down to a you-or-them decision.

One factor to consider is that creditors do not like to write off charges. It's very bad for business, and they take a dim view of those circumstances that require them to do so. With that in mind, reluctance to press charges might be viewed as you being in cahoots with the perpetrator rather than being an innocent victim. Therefore, think long and hard about foregoing charges against your evil twin in this situation.

Chapter 6 Contact All Creditors and Financial Institutions

As already noted, upon learning that you are a victim of identity theft, one of the first things you should do (if not the very first) is contact the financial institutions and creditors with whom you have dealings. You will want to protect the reputation and relationships you have established, and prompt notification will go a long way towards doing that.

(i) Credit cards - Contact each of your credit card issuers and let them know that you have been the victim of identity theft. It is quite likely that, for existing card issuers, there may be legitimate charges intermingled with those that are fraudulent. It will be of immense benefit if you have already gone through your credit card statements and identified the disputed charges. Also, as mentioned earlier, card issuers will, at some point, probably inquire about a police report. In addition, they may also have certain forms of their own that they will ask you to complete, such as affidavits or declarations of fraud.

(ii) Bank accounts - As with credit card issuers, you will want to contact any banks you deal with and let them know that your identity has been compromised. (Fortunately, most of us - although we may have multiple accounts - usually only work with a single bank at a time for checking and savings purposes.) Again, if there are fraudulent charges related to your account, bring those specific items to the bank's attention.

(iii) Other creditors - Falling into this catch-all category will be service providers (e.g., cell phone service), originators of auto loans, and the like. Identity theft in this arena is sometimes a bit more difficult to manage without arousing suspicion - most of us don't pay for cable service in two places, have utilities in our names at two different homes, etc. - but not impossible. For instance, your evil twin may have an additional phone added to your cell phone service, hoping you won't notice what might be a relatively small increase in charges. As before, make these creditors aware of the theft and complete any paperwork they require to investigate the matter.

(iv) New accounts - Contacting new creditors (i.e., creditors with whom your evil twin has opened accounts in your name) is rarely possible to do right away, because you simply don't know who they are. With rare exceptions, you won't find out about unauthorized new accounts until you get a copy of your credit report, so this topic is more fully discussed in the next chapter, and is mentioned here solely for the sake of completeness.

The quickest way to bring the matter of identity theft to the attention of creditors and banks is often via phone or internet, and I would recommend either of those methods first. However, regardless of which approach you ultimately choose (and you might even entertain doing both), you should also follow up with a written letter, which should include the following information, at a minimum:

- Identifying information for the account in question (e.g., account number, account holder, etc.);
- The Incident Report filed with your local police station (including the name of officer in charge and his/her contact information);
- Any documentation required by the institution or creditor, such as affidavits or declarations of fraud;

- A list of the disputed charges or incidents of theft; and
- A request for an estimate of the time necessary for investigation and resolution.

Needless to say, you should maintain a copy of all communications with your creditors and banks.

In terms of additional actions to take, you can always put a freeze on your accounts. Furthermore, you can request that future transactions only be allowed via use of a password. You can also choose to close compromised accounts and open new ones. (No one is saying that these actions are convenient, but they will help you reestablish control over the situation, as well as curtail the amount of damage your evil twin can do.)

For more specific information and resources for each individual state, please visit the Identity Theft Defense HQ website: http://www.identitytheftdefensehq.com/

Chapter 7 Contact Credit Reporting Agencies

In addition to contacting your bank and creditors, you should also contact the three major credit reporting agencies and have them place a fraud alert on your file:

Equifax Consumer Fraud Division
P.O. Box 740256
Atlanta, GA 30374
(800) 525-6285
http://www.equifax.com/answers/set-fraud-alerts/en_cp

Experian Credit Fraud Center
P.O. Box 9554
Allen, TX 75013
(888) 397-3742
https://www.experian.com/fraud/center.html

TransUnion Fraud Victim Assistance Department
P.O. Box 6790, Fullerton, CA 92834
(800) 680-7289
https://www.transunion.com/fraud-victim-resource/fraud-victim-assistance-department

A fraud alert lets creditors know that you may be the victim of identity theft. An initial fraud alert will remain in your credit file for 90 days. (You can also request an extended fraud alert, which will remain in your file for seven years.) Moreover, you typically only have to contact one of the three major agencies, as the first that you contact will inform the other two of your fraud alert.

A fraud alert also entitles you to a free copy of your credit report from each of the three major reporting agencies. It is absolutely critical that you get these, because this is your best - and in some instances, only - means to determine if new credit has been opened in your name. After reviewing your respective credit reports, dispute any incorrect information. Also, request that fraudulent items be hidden or blocked from those viewing your credit report. As to the new creditors, the credit reporting agencies are required to investigate your claims, and any fraudulent information must be removed from your credit report. Moreover, in most instances, you will have no liability for fraudulent new accounts opened without authorization. Still, it may be worthwhile to contact any unauthorized creditors and explain matters to them, including providing them with a copy of the Incident Report.

It will also prove beneficial to contact any local credit reporting agencies. Although Equifax, Experian and TransUnion are usually acknowledged as the three *national* credit reporting agencies, there are smaller local and regional credit reporting agencies in a lot of areas. These are also worthy of your attention when it comes to battling identity theft. Thus, you should also find out the name of the local agency and make sure they are aware of your issues and disputes with respect to fraudulent credit information on your report.

Last but not least, as with corresponding with creditors, it is probably easiest to communicate with credit reporting agencies via phone or online. However, it is probably prudent to follow up any such communications with written correspondence. Such written communication should essentially contain much of the same information that you included in the letters to your creditors (i.e., the Incident Report, the list of disputed charges and fraudulent information, etc.). However, do not forget to include any instructions regarding the placement of a fraud alert in your file, as well as the request for a copy of your credit report.

Chapter 8 Other Agencies to Contact

In addition to the information previously provided in this book, I felt it was worthwhile to point out some of the other resources available to help deal with identity theft:

1) U.S. Postal Inspection Service
Mail Fraud Group
475 L'Enfant Plaza SW, Room 3411
Washington, DC 20260
Tel: 202-268-4267
Fax: 202-268-7316

Mail Fraud Complaint Form:
https://postalinspectors.uspis.gov/forms/MailFraudComplaint.aspx

Please note, per the U.S. Postal Inspection Service website: "Although the Postal Inspection Service cannot resolve routine business disputes between companies and their customers, it can act against a company or individual if there is a pattern of activity suggesting a potential scheme to defraud."

2) Identity Theft Clearinghouse
Federal Trade Commission,
600 Pennsylvania Avenue, NW
Washington, DC 20580
1-877-ID-THEFT (1-877-438-4338)

FTC Identity Theft Complaint Form:
https://www.ftccomplaintassistant.gov/

Please Note, per the FTC's website: "The Federal Trade Commission, the nation's consumer protection agency, collects complaints about companies, business practices, and identity theft under the FTC Act and other laws we enforce or administer...Your complaints can help us detect patterns of wrong-doing, and lead to investigations and prosecutions. The FTC enters all complaints it receives into Consumer Sentinel, a secure online database that is used by thousands of civil and criminal law enforcement authorities worldwide. **The FTC does not resolve individual consumer complaints.**"

3) There are various resources for reporting check fraud, including:

   (i) Telecheck
   (800) 710-9898
   https://www.firstdata.com/content/dam/FirstData/telecheck/telecheck-forgery-identity-theft.html

   (ii) CheckRite
   (800) 766-2748

4) Identity Theft Victims' Statement of Rights: https://www.identitytheft.gov/Know-Your-Rights

5) Lost/Stolen Passports:

U.S. Department of State
Passport Services
Consular Lost/Stolen Passport Section
1111 19th Street, NW, Suite 500
Washington, DC 20036
1-877-487-2778 (TTY 1-888-874-7793)

https://travel.state.gov/content/passports/en/emergencies/lost-or-stolen-passports-abroad.html

6) Social Security Fraud:

Social Security OIG Hotline
P.O. Box 17785
Baltimore, Maryland 21235-7785
1-800-269-0271

http://oig.ssa.gov/report-fraud-waste-or-abuse/fraud-waste-and-abuse

You should not hesitate to make use of any of these resources should the occasion arise. In fact, assuming you are the victim of identity theft, you should consider completion of the Mail Fraud Complaint Form and the FTC Identity Theft Complaint Form as mandatory, as doing so will help bring an end to fraudulent schemes.

EPILOGUE

In closing, it's clear that the best course of action is to try to avoid the possibility of identity theft altogether. Of course, this requires that you be proactive in terms of monitoring your information and taking steps to ensure that it remains safe and secure. The truth of the matter is that everyone has an evil twin out there waiting to come into existence. The trick is to deny them that opportunity, or, barring complete denial, make sure the opportunity is extremely short-lived. Hopefully this book has provided some techniques for prevention of, as well sound advice for recovery from, identity theft. Good luck to you!

THE END

Thank you for purchasing this book. If you found it helpful or enlightening, please feel free to leave a review on the site from which it was purchased.

For additional information on identity theft – including how to combat it and recover from it – please visit my website, Identity Theft Defense HQ, located here: http://www.identitytheftdefensehq.com/

Made in the USA
Monee, IL
05 November 2026

67985533R00025